What's On My Plate?

by RUTH BELOV GROSS

illustrated by ISADORE SELTZER

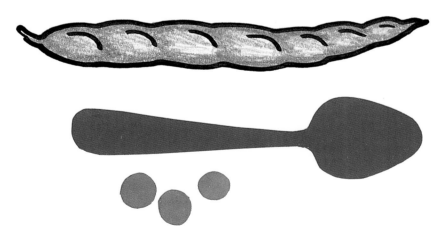

Macmillan Publishing Company   New York

For everyone who loves to eat
and for Balducci's,
where this book began
  — R.B.G.

To tomatoes, potatoes,
chickens, and cows
  — I.S.

Text copyright © 1990 by Ruth Belov Gross
Illustrations copyright © 1990 by Isadore Seltzer
Macmillan
Publishing Company, 866 Third Avenue, New York, NY 10022, Collier Macmillan Canada, Inc.
Printed and bound in Singapore   First American Edition   10 9 8 7 6 5 4 3 2 1

The text of this book is set in 16 point ITC Newtext Light.
The illustrations are mixed media, including colored pencil, acrylic paint, and collage.

Library of Congress Cataloging-in-Publication Data   •   Gross, Ruth Belov.
What's on my plate? Summary: Describes, in simple text and illustrations, where some
of the common things we eat originate. 1. Food — Juvenile literature. [1. Food]
I. Seltzer, Isadore, ill. II. Title.   TX355.G795   1990   641.3   87-22057   ISBN 0-02-737000-3

What's on my plate?
It's applesauce!
Where did it come from?

Applesauce comes from
apples that grow on a tree.

Apple juice
and apple pie
and applesauce
and candied apples
all come from apples
that grow on a tree.

What's on my plate?
Peas!
Where did they come from?

Peas come from pea pods
that grow on a vine.
You open the pea pods
to get the peas out.

Most vines need
something to climb on.
A vine can't stand up by itself.

What's on my plate?
Mashed potatoes!
Where did they come from?
Did they grow on a tree?

Mashed potatoes come from potatoes
that grow in the ground.
Potato chips and French fries
come from potatoes too.

What's in my bowl?
It's cereal!
Where does cereal come from?

Cereal comes from plants that grow in a field—
wheat plants, corn plants, rice plants, and oats.
The seeds are the part that cereal is made from.

Some people put sugar on their cereal.
Sugar comes from plants too—
sugarcane plants and sugar beets.

What's in my hand?
It's a peanut butter and jelly sandwich!
Where did the peanut butter and jelly
come from?

Peanut butter comes from peanuts
that grow in the ground.
The jelly came from grapes
that grew on a vine.

Where did the bread
for my sandwich come from?

Bread begins with
the same plants that
cereal comes from.
The plant seeds are
made into flour.
Then the flour is used
to make bread.

What's on my face?
Where did it come from?

It came from your sandwich, silly.

What's in my hair?
It's popcorn!
Where did it come from?

Popcorn comes from a special
kind of corn called popcorn.
When popcorn seeds get very hot,
they burst open.
Then the inside part pops out.

What's on my plate?
Scrambled eggs!
Where did they come from?

Scrambled eggs come from eggs
that were laid by a chicken.

Scrambled eggs and fried eggs
and hard-boiled eggs and soft-boiled eggs
and egg sandwiches and egg salad
all come from eggs that
were laid by a chicken.

What's on my plate?
A piece of fried chicken!
Where did it come from?

It came from a chicken.

What's in my dish?
It's tuna fish!
Where did it come from?

A tuna is a big fish that swims in the sea.

After it is caught it is cooked
and cut into pieces
and put in little cans.
It doesn't look like a big fish after that.

What's in my hand?

Raisins!

Where did they come from?

Raisins started out as grapes.
Then they were put in the sun to dry.
The sun turned the juicy grapes
into wrinkled raisins.

What was in my cup just now?
   Where did it come from—
      and where did it go?

There was milk in your cup—
and now it's in you!
Milk comes from cows who
eat grass in the meadow.

If we didn't get
milk from cows,
we wouldn't have
ice cream
or butter
or cheese.
All of them are
made from milk.

Now what's on my face?

It's strawberry jam!
Strawberry jam comes from strawberries
that grow close to the ground.

What's in my glass?
Orange juice!
Where did it come from?

Orange juice comes from oranges
that grow on a tree.
When you squeeze the oranges,
you get orange juice.

What's in my dish?
It's chocolate pudding!
Where did it come from?

The chocolate in chocolate pudding
comes from beans that
grow on cocoa trees.
Chocolate pudding
has milk and sugar in it too.

Cocoa trees grow
in hot countries.
Cocoa beans grow
inside of cocoa pods.

Chocolate pudding
and chocolate bars
and chocolate cake
and chocolate icing
and hot chocolate
and chocolate milk
are all made with
chocolate that comes
from cocoa trees.

CHOCO

What's on my bun?
It's a hamburger!
Where did it come from?

Hamburgers come from cows and steers.
Their meat is called beef.
The butcher grinds the beef up
to make hamburger meat.

Cows and steers are called cattle.

What's on my hamburger?
It's catsup!
Where did it come from?

Catsup comes from tomatoes
that grow in the sun.

What's in the jar?
It's a pickle!
Where did it come from?

It came from a cucumber.
Cucumbers grow on vines
on the ground.
You need vinegar to make
pickles out of cucumbers.

Vinegar is made from apples,
grapes, rice, and other things
that people eat.
It tastes sour.

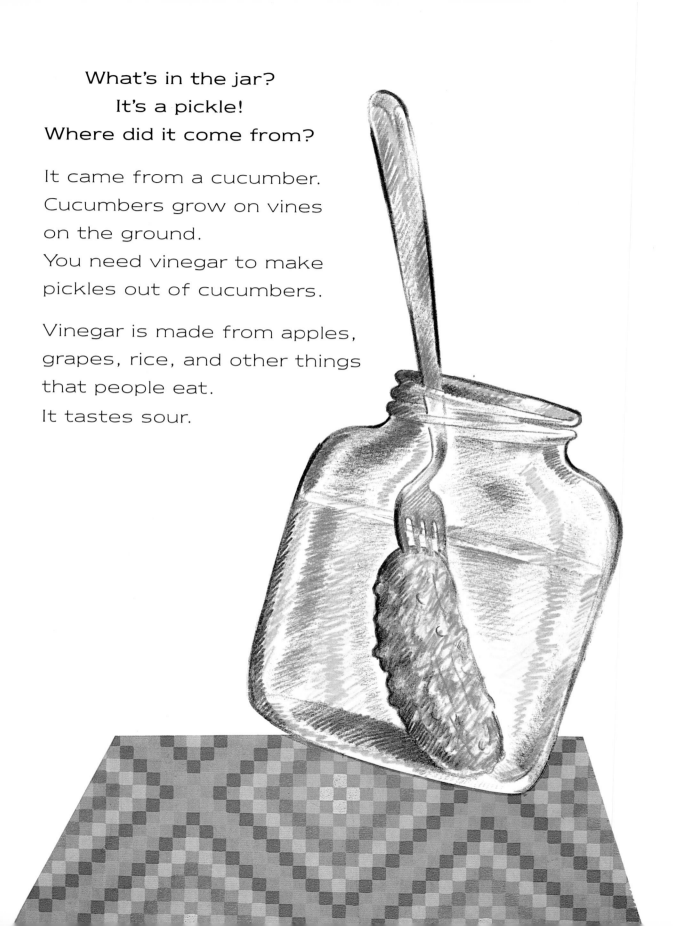

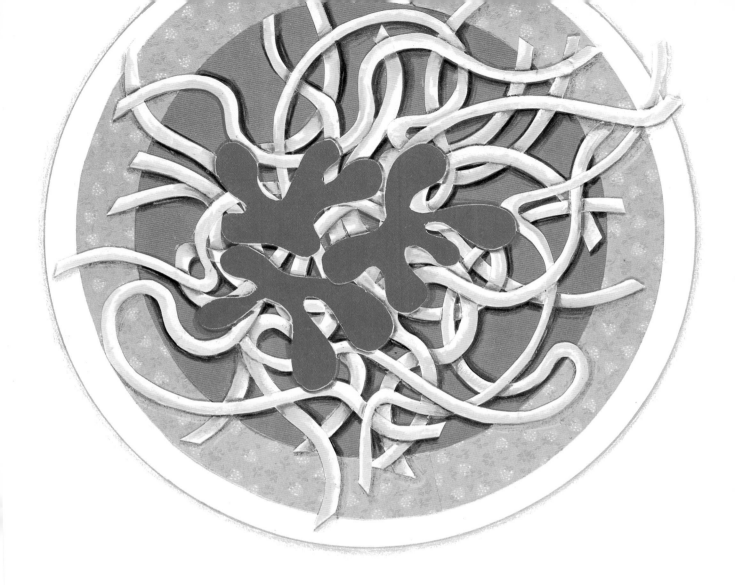

What's on my shirt?
It's spaghetti!
Where did it come from?

The red part comes from tomato sauce.
Tomato sauce is something like catsup.
The spaghetti part was made with flour.
Spaghetti flour comes from wheat plants.

What's in the pot?
It's soup!
Where did it come from?

Soup comes from all the good things
you put into it.
Tomato soup comes from tomatoes
that grow in the sun.
Pea soup comes from peas
that grow on a vine.
Potato soup comes from potatoes
that grow in the ground.
And chicken soup comes from chickens!
You can make soup out of
almost anything you want.

What's on the table?
It's your birthday cake!

It has eggs in it
that were laid by a chicken.
It has milk and butter in it
from cows in the meadow.
It has flour and sugar in it
from plants in the field.
And it has chocolate
that came from cocoa trees.

Everything we eat
was once part of a plant
or came from an animal.